THEN AND THERE P9-DTQ-897

GENERAL EDITOR

MARJORIE REEVES, M.A., PH.D.

Ancient Crete and Mycenae

JAMES BOLTON, M.A.

Illustrated from contemporary sources

LONGMAN

LONGMAN GROUP LIMITED
London

Associated companies, branches and representatives
throughout the world

© Longman Group Ltd (formerly
Longmans, Green & Co Ltd) 1968

First published 1968
Fourth impression 1973

ISBN 0 582 20415 1

FOR RICHARD AND MATTHEW

ACKNOWLEDGEMENTS

For permission to reproduce copyright drawings and photographs, we
are indebted to the following:–British Museum–pages 2, 77 and 87; British
School at Athens–pages 25 (bottom); Cambridge University Press–pages
4 and 78; Hirmer Fotoarchiv–pages 8, 14, 16, 17 (priestess), 18, 25 (top),
26, 33, 34 and 35, 36, 37, 38 and 39, 40 and 41, 43, 44, 50, 57, 61 (both),
62 (both), 63, 70, 74 (three) and 86; Macmillan & Co. Ltd., (Mrs. Wace)
pages 72 and 73; Macmillan and Co. Ltd.–pages 83 and 84; Mansell
Collection–pages 32 and 90; Ministry of Works, Crown Copyright–page 1;
Pendlebury Parish (*Handbook of the Palaces of Minos and Knossos*)–page 6;
Penguin Publications–pages 17 (left), 29 (both), 79 and 81; Piet de Jong–
pages 7 and 59, Princeton University Press–pages 19, 20, 21, 28 (both),
and 45 (both); Royal Ontario Museum, University of Toronto–pages 15;
Drawing after E. Sjoguist–page 30; University of Cincinnati–page 71.

Printed in Hong Kong by
The Hong Kong Printing Press Ltd.

CONTENTS

TO THE READER

In this book you will find not the story but the picture of two peoples. These peoples lived more than three thousand years ago in what we now call Crete and Greece. They were the first people in Europe to build great palaces and enjoy what is called civilisation. They were also the first Europeans to read and write, as you will see. But they have left no books of history and so we cannot tell their story. But from the remains they left behind, which have been dug out of the earth, we can make a picture of them and of their way of life.

In this book you will find that the pictures have as much to tell you as the words, for in most cases they are photographs of the actual buildings these ancient people lived in and of the very things they used. In some cases the pictures are called 'reconstructions' or 'restorations'. This means that an artist has put all the information together that archaeologists can give him and used it to make a painting of the palaces as they were over three thousand years ago. Sometimes you will find two pictures of the same room or building, one a view of the place as it is now, the other a restoration. Compare these and you will begin to see how the artist has set about his task.

Many books have been written about Crete and Greece, and often they have wonderful pictures. See if you can find one or two at your local library. One of the finest is 'Crete and Mycenae' by Marinatos and Hirmer. See also if you can find a book with the stories or myths of the ancient Greeks. Better still buy the translation of the 'Odyssey' by E. V. Rieu in the Penguin series; there you will find a real story and a wonderful adventure. Some day too you will perhaps be able to go to Greece and sail the seas that Odysseus sailed; you will see the land of Agamemnon and the island of Minos, and visit the great museums of Athens and Heraklion where their treasures are still to be seen.

Words printed in *italics* are explained in the Glossary.

I Minos and the Labyrinth

'There is a land called Crete set in the middle of the wine-dark
sea; beautiful it is and fertile, and the sea flows all around. On
it dwell men too many to count, and there are ninety cities.
One of these is Knossos, a great city, where for nine years
ruled King Minos.' So wrote Homer, the earliest of Greek
poets, more than seven hundred years before the birth of
Christ. Minos and his kingdom were little more than *legends* to
the Greeks, and this is not surprising, for the great palaces of
Crete were destroyed some seven hundred years before the
time of Homer around 1400 B.C. The stories lingered on long
after the palaces had collapsed, when the sites where they
once had stood were little hills covered with grass and bushes
with here and there a few half-hidden blocks of masonry and a
scattering of broken pieces of pottery.

Many were the stories the Greeks told about Minos. They
said that he was the first ruler of the seas, the first king to have a
fleet powerful enough to subdue the pirates of the Greek seas
and so make them safe for his traders. Minos was also a law-
giver and a friend of the gods of heaven, but above all he was a
builder. His most famous building was a great *maze* called the
Labyrinth. Have you ever seen the maze at Hampton Court? It
looks like this:

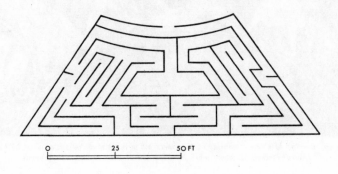

You will see that it is a kind of puzzle made of paths, and the idea is to get to the centre without getting lost. The maze of Minos was a tangle of dark passages and was so cunningly built that no one who did not know its secret could escape from it. At the heart of the Labyrinth was the den of a monstrous man-eating beast, half man and half bull, called the Minotaur.

At that time, so the story goes, Minos had power over many cities on the mainland of Greece. One of these cities, Athens, had caused the death of his son, and in revenge for this Minos claimed a savage tribute. Every eight years seven boys and seven girls had to be sent to Crete as victims for the Minotaur. One year Theseus, the son of the king of Athens, demanded to be sent as one of the seven boys; he wanted to save his city from this cruel burden. When he arrived in Crete he happened to meet Ariadne, the beautiful daughter of King Minos. She was enchanted by Theseus' courage and beauty and promised to help him, if only he would rescue her from her father's palace and take her back to Greece with him. He agreed, and

Theseus and the Minotaur: painting on the underneath of a cup made in Athens about 520 B.C.
Theseus conceals his sword while the Minotaur prepares to hurl a huge boulder

secretly she gave him the two things he needed, a sword and a ball of thread. Theseus was the first of the Minotaur's victims that year to be thrust into the Labyrinth, there to wander in the maze without hope of escape until he finally stumbled on the monster's lair in the centre. But Theseus, hiding his sword, carefully unwound the thread as he made his way through the windings of the maze. In the lair at the heart of the Labyrinth Theseus slew the Minotaur among the bones of his former victims. Then tracing his way back along the thread, he escaped from the maze, found Ariadne and his companions and set sail for Athens. There we must leave the world of legend and turn to the island itself.

Crete is a small mountainous island surrounded, as Homer said, by the beautiful deep blue of the eastern Mediterranean. It is a narrow island, never more than about thirty-six miles wide, and the mountains stretch almost unbroken for the 160 miles of its length. But in the plains the land is very fertile and will grow good crops of wheat and barley. Vines and olive trees also do well, and we shall see that the ancient Cretans grew rich by trading in wine and olive oil. The two largest of the small fertile plains are in the centre of the island; one is in the north near the modern town of Heraklion, the other, lying almost due south, is the plain of the Mesara. It is easy to go from one of these plains to the other, and the agriculture in them has always provided most of the island's wealth. In the crops they grow and how they trade, the life of the people of Crete has not changed very much since the days of Minos thousands of years ago.

Seventy years ago the Crete of King Minos was no more than a land of legend. No one knew that the palaces and towns of ancient Crete lay buried beneath the soil, soil that as often as not was planted with wheat or olive trees. The greatest of all the Cretan palaces, the palace of Knossos, was discovered by an English *archaeologist*, Sir Arthur Evans. He was attracted

3

Three-sided seal-stone from Crete. This shows the sort of picture signs that attracted Evans. Can you say what any of them are?

to Crete because he was fascinated by a kind of small precious stone, beautifully carved, that was said to come from there. Have you seen a signet ring? It has a carved stone which, when pressed into wax or clay, leaves its picture behind. We use them to seal important papers. These ancient carved stones were also used for making such pictures and so are called seal stones.

Evans was fascinated by these stones because some of them seemed to him to carry a kind of picture writing, like the picture writing of the Egyptians, which had only been *deciphered* some fifty years previously. Evans arrived in Crete in 1894. He learned that large numbers of seal stones together with a great deal of broken pottery had been found on a low hill a few miles to the south of Heraklion. More exciting still a Cretan (named Minos surprisingly enough) had dug some trenches there and found a number of *massive* stone walls and a store of huge jars. Evans was now sure that he had found a site where there was much to be discovered, and at once set about buying as much of it as he could. All the same, at that time he could have had no idea of the treasures that lay below the surface of that low and apparently unexciting hill, which we now call Knossos.

In 1894 the Turks still ruled Crete, and Evans was not able to buy the rest of the site and begin digging for another five years, till in 1899 the Turks handed the island of Crete back to Greece. The task that faced Evans was vast and compli-

4

cated. The site stretched over an area of three acres or more. What he was looking for was buried under the surface of the soil, and at the same time he had no idea of what he might expect to find. Can you imagine him standing and wondering where to dig the first spadeful?

When an archaeologist *excavates* a site he has one main principle to guide him: the further you dig downwards, the further you go back in time. So you begin by digging a trench taking great care to keep the sides of the trench *vertical*. Then as you go down, if you are lucky, you can see the different stages in the development of the site stacked neatly one on top of the other. When your trench reaches a wall, then you can follow the wall along by digging the earth away. But supposing you find, as Evans did, that the wall you are tracing belongs not to the ground floor but to an upper storey, what do you do then? If you preserve the upper storey, you never find out what happened on the ground floor; but if you dig down to the ground floor, you are bound to destroy the remains of the upper storey. In the end Evans decided to replace the ancient floors and beams of the upper stories, where he could find clear proof of them, with modern constructions of steel and reinforced concrete, built to match the ancient work as closely as possible. So the palace of Knossos as we see it today is in part restored, and indeed the restorations make it much easier to picture the palace as it was in the days of its greatness 3,400 years ago.

The Cretans who lived at Knossos are often called Minoans after King Minos. They planned their palaces round a great *rectangular* court. This always ran from north to south, and at Knossos it is about 80 feet broad by 170 feet long. Around this rose the palace buildings in most parts two stories high, but in some parts rising to three stories. To our eyes, accustomed to high skyscrapers, the palace would have seemed to be a low group of buildings with flat roofs, sprawling rather shapelessly

5

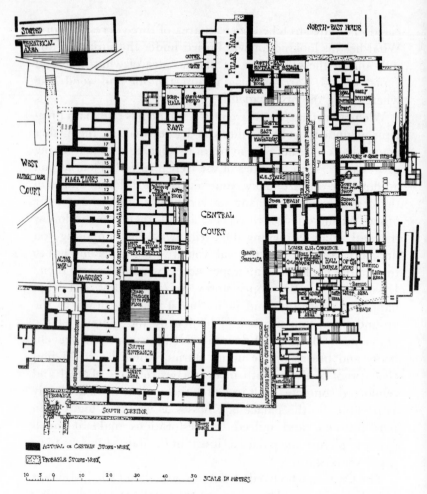

Plan of the Palace at Knossos

over the ground. But the palaces were in fact carefully planned.
The buildings along the two long sides of the central court, the
east side and the west side, had quite different parts to play in
the working of the palace. In the buildings to the east of the
court were the living quarters, while to the west were the state

6

The west side of the Central Court, Knossos; an imaginary restoration. See if you can work out where this picture fits into the plan on p. 6.

rooms, great halls for the reception of state visitors, and smaller rooms where the *rites* of the mysterious Cretan religion were performed.

In ancient Crete a palace was much more than the ruler's home. Of course it had to house the king and his family and a very large number of slaves. Probably a number of noble men and women would also live in the palace to attend on the king and queen. But the kingdom would also be ruled from the palace. The scribes who kept the records of dues and taxes would have their offices in the palace, and might even live there. The taxes, moreover, would actually be paid into the palace, and as the kings of Crete lived nearly a thousand years before money was invented, the taxes had to be paid 'in kind' —that is, in actual produce, bushels of corn or measures of wine and olive oil. As we shall see later, clay tablets belonging to the Cretan record offices were discovered by Evans at Knossos, and the long corridor of store-rooms with its huge jars that had been used for storing grain or liquid is today one of the best preserved and most intriguing parts of the palace.

7

The Grand Staircase: this is the lower part of the staircase; to the left is the light well rising to the level of the Central Court

The corridor with its store-rooms naturally belonged to the western, the official side of the palace. But the eastern side has its surprises as well. North of the living quarters were large numbers of small workrooms. There the palace potters, metal workers, jewellers, carpenters and other craftsmen worked. This is proved by the bits and pieces found in these rooms, chippings of stone and ivory, lumps of raw metal, stores of pottery, as well as things that the craftsmen never completed.

At Knossos today the ruins of the palace are almost all that remains to be seen. There are, of course, remains of other buildings, mostly private houses belonging to men associated with the palace, but they are only a small fraction of the town that must once have surrounded it. Various guesses at the size of the population of this town have been made; Evans thought it might have been as large as 80,000, but nowadays archaeologists think that a figure half that size is more likely to be right. Even so, Knossos was a large town for those days. However, its streets and houses are likely to remain buried as they are under the farm land of Crete. Sometimes, of course, a farmer ploughing a field to a greater depth than usual comes across ancient pieces of building and the archaeologists are able to investigate, but this is a slow and *inefficient* way of uncovering a whole town. It is to the palace that we must look for our picture of the ancient Cretans, remembering that the palace could not have existed without the town that surrounded it.

We have seen how many different activities went on in the palace buildings. Look again at the plan of the palace with its hundreds of rooms and corridors surrounding the great court, its staircases leading up from the court and on the east side down to two floors of state apartments below the level of the court. The plan is almost unbelievably complicated; it was a building in which a stranger could easily lose himself. It was indeed a labyrinth. Now the word 'labyrinth' comes from

9

'labrys' which means a 'double-axe', and so 'labyrinth' will mean 'House of the Double-axe'. The double-axe was a sacred object in the Cretan religion. In the palace of Knossos the sign of the double-axe is constantly to be found carved on the pillars.

This for us is the first place at Knossos where the facts and the legends meet. The great palace with its pillars carved with the sacred symbol was indeed the 'House of the Double-axe', the Labyrinth—and a labyrinth it must have been in our sense of the word to strangers from the mainland of Greece at a time when such buildings were quite unknown on the mainland. You can imagine a Greek trader, perhaps, getting lost in the corridors and wandering round and round. It was the Greeks who called it a labyrinth and gave the word its modern meaning of a confusing tangle of paths or passages where you can easily lose your way. This then was how the legend of Theseus and the Minotaur started. How well the rest of the legend fits in with what has been discovered we must see as we examine the various parts of the palace, building up as we go a picture of the life of the ancient Cretans.

2   At Home in the Labyrinth

When a building has lain in ruins for over three thousand years, it is not easy to imagine it as it once was, full of colour and life. At Knossos we are helped as we try to picture the palace as it used to be by the lie of the land. On the eastern side of the central court the ground slopes steeply down to the stream, Kairatos. The *architects* used this slope when they came to build the main living rooms of the palace. They cut into the slope of the hill below the level of the central court; the outside of this cutting they supported with a great *retaining wall*, and so provided enough level ground for a magnificent set of private rooms. The floor of this cutting is nearly thirty feet below the surface of the central court, and so the Minoans were able to have groups of living rooms on two stories below the level of the court. To reach these rooms they constructed a monumental staircase running down from the court.

In buildings as old as the palace of Minos it is rare for anything more than a few of the lowest *courses* of walls to survive, and staircases to an upper storey are practically never found. But at Knossos, as the staircase is built on the downward slope of the hill, it survived, while the two uppermost stories of the palace—built above the level of the central court—collapsed. Indeed the wreckage of the upper stories filled the lower flights of the stairs, while the wooden beams and pillars of the staircase were still sound. When in course of time the beams and pillars rotted away, this wreckage rammed tight together supported the structure of the stairs.

Evans came upon the staircase in the course of excavating the rooms and corridors that lie immediately to the north of it. He was not expecting to find a staircase, and his surprise was all the greater when he found that the flights of stairs led both down and up. Naturally he wanted to follow the stairs down as far as they led, but to do this would have meant digging down through the flight of stairs that led upwards; it would have meant destroying the upper part of the stairs, and this, of course, he did not want to do. It was fortunate that he had among his workmen some miners from the ancient mining town of Laurion on the mainland of Greece. They were able to tunnel along the great staircase supporting it with wooden props as they went. (They used miners' pit props.) Even so it was a difficult and dangerous operation. The wooden pillars which had originally supported the stairs could still be traced, but only as charred and powdery black dust, and in spite of the props the whole structure often threatened to collapse. In the end four flights of stairs, fifty-five steps in all, were uncovered. Evans decided that this magnificent discovery must somehow be preserved.

The beams and pillars of cypress wood were replaced in modern materials, mostly steel and concrete, shaped and painted to imitate the original structure. Some of the steps had settled below their original position and these had to be raised and held in place until the new columns could be put in to carry the load. If you look carefully at the picture, you will notice that the columns *taper* downwards; they are wider at the top than at the bottom. No one knows why the Cretans tapered their columns in this way, but most probably it was because they liked the shape. The steps themselves were made not of wood but of gypsum. This is a beautiful gleaming white stone, that is also very soft and easy to work. The Minoans, who, of course, only had bronze saws and chisels, used gypsum rather as we use marble, when they wanted to make floors or walls of some particularly splendid material.

The staircase bends back on itself like a letter U: the space to the west of the U is a shaft running right down through the building and open at the top to let in light and air. These shafts, which are called light wells, are found in the palaces of Crete wherever rooms needed light and ventilation. The Cretans had no window glass, and the climate then, as now, is very hot in summer, but often stormy with very high winds in winter. A window opening directly to the outside would make the rooms uncomfortably hot in summer and draughty in winter. But the light well leaves the room cool in summer and still in winter, because it takes in light and air well above the level of the room it serves and neither sun nor wind beats directly onto the room.

Many visitors to Knossos find that the Palace comes most vividly to life as they walk down the four flights of the great staircase. The wide shallow steps seem to conjure up a procession of courtiers, men and women dressed in the elaborate and colourful costumes, that we know so well from wall-paintings. The Palace seems to belong not to the excavators of the twentieth century, but to these ghosts, which our imagination has conjured out of the ancient stones.

From the foot of the stairs a narrow corridor leads to the largest and most magnificent of the reception rooms. This great hall is about 40 feet long and 26 feet wide. At one end of it is another light-well and at the other a *portico*, which opens onto a little terrace. The pillars of the light well have carved on them in many places the sacred symbol of the double-axe, and so Evans gave it the resounding name 'Hall of the Double Axes'. In the middle of one of the walls a wooden throne was placed. Above the throne a spiral pattern was painted on the plaster surface, running along the wall. Probably great shields made of layer upon layer of ox-hide stretched over a wooden frame were hung on the wall along the spiral pattern.

The hall was divided into two by a row of five rectangular pillars. Panels were let into the sides of these pillars to allow doors to be folded back flush with the pillars. In fact the Cretans had over 3,000 years ago what we now call a 'room divider' The same arrangement of double doors was used to shut off the outer part of the hall from the L-shaped verandah.

The Hall of the Double-Axes: a view looking towards the light well at the inside (west) end of the Hall

In all there were no less than eleven sets of double doors, which the occupants of the Hall of the Double Axes could open or shut, either to control draughts and temperature or to cut themselves off from other people.

This room was probably used by the king and his courtiers in their leisure time. From it a narrow passage led turning a right-angled corner to a smaller room. This room has light wells on two sides, and on a third side a small bathroom. Its walls were decorated with fine paintings of dancers and dolphins, and there can be little doubt that this was the Queen's Hall. The queen and her ladies-in-waiting used this room just as the king and his men used the Hall of the Double-Axes. Do not think, though, that men were excluded from the Queen's Hall; it is much too close to the men's hall, and nothing we know about the Minoans suggests that they would have shut their women up in separate women's quarters.

The Queen's Hall (restoration) : below the dolphin painting are two doors; the one on the left leads to the Hall of the Double Axes, the one on the right to a private staircase to the floor above

Let us take a closer look at the paintings of the Queen's Hall. The most vivid of them is the seascape of dolphins and smaller fishes. Around the frame of the picture are prickly sea urchins and streamers of what looks like sea weed are trailed in between the swimming fish. The fish themselves are marvellously well drawn; fins, eyes, tails, the dolphins' snouts, all are full of movement and life. Elaborate patterns of *spirals* and *rosettes* cover the ceiling and the sides of the columns. On one of these the head and shoulders of a lady of the court have been preserved. Her hair is drawn floating out on either side of her in long plaits to show that she is dancing. Of course, when they were found the pictures consisted of small fragments of painted plaster. After so many centuries they naturally lay jumbled in hopeless confusion. Trying to piece the pictures together again is an extraordinarily difficult task. It is like doing a vast jigsaw puzzle the size of a wall with more than half the pieces missing, and the pieces that are left have crumbling edges and

The Queen's Hall as it is now: the paintings have been restored.

faded colours. When the pieces had been fitted together to the best of the archaeologists' ability, Evans got two Swiss artists to fill in the missing parts of the pictures. But ideas about what was missing could differ widely. Evans had one painting restored to show a boy picking fruit; archaeologists now think that the boy was in fact a monkey.

Originally the walls of all the important rooms and corridors were covered with paintings, but, as you would expect, only a small fraction of the original paintings have survived. Some of the scenes represented processions of officials, guards and tribute bearers. At the head of one of these processions comes the splendid figure of a young prince. He wears nothing but a pair of elaborate trunks, also, as we shall see, worn by the bull jumpers, and a magnificent head-dress with long feathers arching out behind and falling forward over his forehead. He has long hair streaming out behind, but at the front it is dressed in careful ringlets that peep out from under his head-dress. No less splendid than the young prince is the head and shoulders

The Young Prince from Knossos

Young Priestess from Knossos
(the Petite Parisienne)

of a young priestess, whom Evans called the 'petite Parisienne'
—or little girl from Paris. She earns her nickname with her
fashionable eye make-up and bright red lipstick. You can see
too that her hair is very carefully waved and set, and it is tied
with a great ceremonial knot as it tumbles down her neck. It is
this knot that shows that she is a priestess.

Minoan pottery was also brilliantly painted. Sometimes the
painter recorded the sea creatures, especially octopuses, that
Minoan sailors must have known so well, and octopus was
certainly a favourite food in ancient Crete just as it is in modern
Greece. Sometimes we find a pattern of papyrus plants, and
one vase from Phaistos has a brilliant pattern of grasses,
beautifully drawn and just right for the jug on which it is

17

Octopus Vase from East Crete: this splendid creature was painted about 1500 B.C. Notice his suckers and the pieces of sea weed

painted. You can see this on page 90. The Minoan painter had a keen eye and a wonderful feeling for setting down what he saw simply, directly and with great delicacy of touch.

As we saw before, the Queen's Hall has a bathroom leading off it. This was a small room little more than seven feet square. It was separated from the bigger room by a low wall supporting two pillars. Of course, to make the bathroom more private curtains or hangings could have been draped between the pillars; on the other hand the Minoans may not have thought it necessary, as we do today, to take one's bath in private. In Homer's time guests who arrived at a nobleman's house were helped with their bathing by a daughter of the house.

Although, as we shall see, Minoan plumbing was very advanced, the baths did not have hot and cold piped water. They used portable clay bathtubs, big enough to sit in quite comfortably, for they were four feet or more in length. Slaves brought water in pitchers, and may have poured it over the person taking a bath. The baths were made with handles, so that they could be carried out and emptied down a drain, and some bathrooms were even provided with a drain in the floor.

Another narrow corridor leads out of the Queen's Hall to a number of even more private rooms to the west (that is nearer the Great Court). One of these, to the surprise and delight of visitors to the Palace, was a lavatory. This has clear traces of a wooden seat and was flushed straight down to a large stone drain. There was also a device which seems to have been designed to prevent smells coming back from the drain. This

The 'Queen's Bathroom' (restoration): a view over the low wall that separates the bathroom from the 'Queen's Hall'

drain ran in a loop beneath the floors of the rooms we have been describing. It collected rain water from five light wells;

water from the roof and probably also served lavatories on the upper floors, in addition to the one near the Queen's Hall. The drain was built of stone blocks lined with cement, and as the drain passage measured 31 by 15 inches, men could enter it through manholes specially provided, when it needed cleaning.

Water pipes from Knossos

The Palace also had some sort of piped water supply, though we do not know in detail how it worked or where the water came from. The pipes, which have been found beneath the floors, were made of clay in lengths of 2–2½ feet. Each section had a *flange* which enabled it to be cemented firmly to the next length of pipe, and, as you can see from the drawing, every section tapered sharply in the direction of the flow of water. This taper made the water shoot through the narrow sections more quickly, and this will have helped to flush any *sediment* along the pipe and keep it clear of obstructions.

The Minoans then were wealthy and ingenious, and they used both their money and their brains to make their living rooms as comfortable as possible. Unfortunately we cannot bring the rooms fully to life without the furniture, hangings, rugs and ornaments, that must once have been there; and these have not survived. Wall-paintings and carved gemstones give us an idea of their folding stools and chairs. There must have been tables and beds, but these, too, have not survived. We are luckier when we come to the kitchen equipment, because it was made of clay. The Minoans did not have fixed hearths. Instead they used portable *tripod* hearths for heating, and a great variety of portable ovens and grills for cooking. The oven you can see in the picture had two halves. The lower half was for the fuel, probably charcoal, and the top half was designed to allow the food to be cooked for a long time at an even temperature. Little grill and spit supports were used to hold skewers piercing a number of pieces of meat. The result was probably like the *kebabs* you can get in restaurants in England, or the 'souflakhia' (made of tiny little pieces of meat) that you can buy from little roadside shops in Greece.

But now we must leave the living rooms of the Palace, climb back up the Grand Staircase, and cross the Central Court to the state rooms on its west side.

Portable Oven (front view and back view)

3   Trade and the Throne

At first glance the view across the Central Court is disappointing. You see a long, rather muddled, range of buildings, and much of what you see has obviously been rebuilt in modern reinforced concrete. The plan in your guide-book is not much more help. It shows a confusing jumble of small rooms; behind this jumble there is a long corridor running north and south, and running back from the corridor eighteen long, narrow storage rooms called 'magazines'. Where, you may wonder, are the state rooms to be found?

On the east side of the Palace the slope of the hill allowed the architect to place the main rooms one or two stories below the level of the Central Court. On the west side there was no such slope, and the main rooms must have been one storey up from the Court. So we see at Knossos, just to the right of the centre of the range of buildings, a staircase some thirteen feet wide. Two round blocks of stone must have supported pillars in the centre of the staircase. A staircase as grand as this must have led to rooms of importance. In fact there were probably three great halls placed side by side with windows looking over the outer west court towards the setting sun. The largest of these was about 57 by 51 ft, and so would have been big enough for the most splendid of court functions, such as welcoming ambassadors from foreign kings.

Immediately to the south of the staircase on ground level was a group of rooms devoted to the worship of the Cretan gods and goddesses. On the edge of the Court stood a low shrine of columns topped by a curious pattern of horns. Only the faintest traces of this shrine were found by the excavators, but they were enough to convince Sir Arthur Evans that the building here must be like one shown in a miniature wall painting of which fragments had been found in another part of

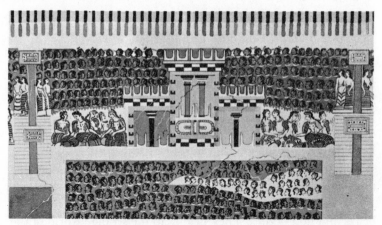

Crowd painting from Knossos: women occupy the seats of honour next to the shrine

the palace. This is the painting you can see in the illustration.
The shrine is in the centre of a great crowd of people, who are
probably watching a display—perhaps the bull-jumping
sport—but nobody is watching from the shrine itself, so the
columns and the pattern of horns can be seen quite clearly.
We shall see later on that this pattern probably represents
bull's horns, which were for the Minoans a sacred symbol.

To the left of the shrine a short flight of steps leads down to a
little open court. On the other side of this court are two small
rooms with large square pillars in the centre. As we have come
down from the Central Court these rooms are half underground, and so have been called 'pillar *crypts*'. The pillars are
made of four blocks of stone making the total height of these
crypts only 5 ft 9 in. Almost every face of the pillars is marked
with the ⋋, the sacred sign of the double-axe. At the foot
of one of the pillars are two stone-lined basins. These were to
catch liquid offerings poured in *libation* to the gods. These
basins in the small dark underground crypts may suggest
offerings of blood, but it is more likely that wine or olive oil, or
even honey, was poured in libation before these sacred pillars.

23

To the right of the shrine four openings separated by square stone pillars lead down a flight of four broad steps to another suite of sacred rooms. We pass through an anteroom with benches round the walls into the famous Room of the Throne. On the right in a gap between the stone benches that line the walls of the room you can see the oldest throne in Europe. The throne, as you can see in the picture, is a simple chair with a high back standing on a low platform. The high back has wavy sides' and the seat is hollowed out, so that although the throne is made of *alabaster* it is very comfortable to sit on. The walls of the Room of the Throne are painted with a row of griffins. Griffins are imaginary monsters with bird beaks and lion bodies. They belong to the strange world of the Minoan gods and goddesses. Here the two griffins crouched on either side of the throne seem to be watching over it, to protect whoever sat on it, whether king, priest or priestess.

Opposite the throne is a low wall overlooking a small sunken room (rather like the bathroom next to the Queen's Hall). This half-underground room is reached by a small flight of steps in the far corner of the Room of the Throne. It must have been used for religious ceremonies. Perhaps the Minoans believed that when the priest or priestess went down into the earth he would gain power from this close contact with the spirits of the earth. We do know that on the day the palace was destroyed ceremonies were being performed in the Room of the Throne. Large flat stone vases were found scattered over the floor and nearby were the remains of a great storage jar which cannot have belonged in this room. It is not hard to imagine the priests taking oil from this jar and pouring libations from the stone vases in a frantic effort to save the doomed palace from destruction.

To reach the corridor of the magazines we leave the Central Court by a narrow corridor next to the Room of the Throne, and after a couple of sharp right-angled turns find ourselves at

The Room of the Throne, Knossos

The Room of the Throne, Knossos (restored): this picture shows the sunken room on the left. In the room beyond can be seen the figure of a goddess between gold double-axes. Why has the artist put those stone vases in the foreground?

The Corridor of the Magazines, Knossos: the pits in the magazines were also used for storage. Beyond the magazines is the West Court

the north end of the corridor which runs the whole length of the palace. The magazines (eighteen were still in use in the last days of the palace) are to our right. None of them are more than eight feet wide, and they vary in length from about 35 to 60 feet. In many of them the huge Minoan storage jars are still standing intact. Some of these jars are as much as seven feet in height, so Ali Baba's thieves would have found it quite easy to hide in them. The jars were nearly all used for storing olive oil, though some were used for grain, beans, peas and lentils. The average jar could hold about 29 gallons, and there was storage space for about 420 jars. This would mean that the royal storerooms at Knossos could have held well over 12,000 gallons of oil.

Why should the kings of Knossos have wanted to store such vast amounts of oil? We must remember that all through ancient times olive oil was used much more than it is today.

Of course it was used in great quantities for cooking, as it is in Mediterranean countries today. It had in fact to serve as butter, margarine and cooking fat. But it was also used to give light. The ancients didn't use candles, instead they used lamps like the one in the picture on p. 19, with oil for fuel and a nozzle to hold the wick, which was probably made of wool. In addition to this, oil was used as a substitute for soap when people had baths. Oil was rubbed all over the body and the mixture of oil and dirt later scraped off by a special comb-like instrument, which the Romans called a 'strigil'.

Oil, then, was very important to the people of Ancient Crete, and indeed to all the people of that time. But the oil store at Knossos could hold far more oil than the palace and town of Knossos could possibly use themselves. So you can see that the kings of Knossos must have exported large quantities of oil. Besides being kings they were also merchants, and the long row of magazines was their warehouse. And the magazines were more than a warehouse. The Minoans lived long before the invention of coined money; all their trade had to be carried on by *barter*, that is by exchanging one sort of goods (for instance oil) against another (gold or ivory). Merchants of later times stored their wealth, as gold or silver coins, in treasure chests or banks. The wealth of the kings of Knossos was their oil, and so the magazines were both warehouse and store of treasure.

We can see from another palace, the one at Mallia, how carefully the Minoans looked after their oil. Here the oil-store was a block of six magazines, which could only be entered through a single door. The magazines were smaller than those at Knossos with a total capacity of about 158 jars. The jars stood against the two long walls of the magazines on a low cement platform. These platforms have a system of furrows and channels which empty into jars buried up to their neck in the floor at the end of each magazine. This was a way of

27

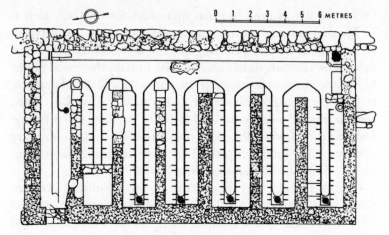

0 1 2 3 4 5 6 METRES

Plan of the Magazines at Mallia

making sure that no oil was wasted by spilling. The large storage jars had to be filled by hand from smaller jars (amphorae), and standing on their platform their mouths will have been as much as eight or nine feet above floor level. A little round clay stool, with hand-holes for carrying, was found in the magazines of another palace. Anybody less than six foot high would have needed it when trying to fill or empty these vast jars. In one corner of the magazine corridor at Mallia is a block of stone. This may have been the place where the overseer sat making a record of all the oil coming into or leaving the store. We shall see later that the palace authorities both in Crete and on the mainland of Greece kept very careful accounts.

0 1 FT

Clay Stool

It is always a good thing for a trader, even if he is a king, to keep his accounts carefully. But whom did the kings of Knossos trade with, and what means of transport did they have? In the days before the coming of the railways water transport was always

28

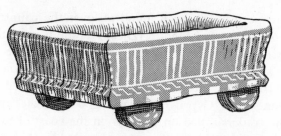

*Waggon: this clay model shows the clumsy solid wheels very clearly.
It may have been a child's toy*

the easiest and most efficient way of carrying goods in bulk.
We know many of the places to which Cretan traders went
because archaeologists can recognise Cretan pottery when
they dig it up. You probably think that wood and iron are
much stronger than cups and jugs. You know what happens
if you hit a vase with either end of a hammer; you throw the
bits of pottery away and put the hammer quickly back in the
tool-box. But in a thousand years' time what will the archaeologist find? He won't find the hammer because the metal will
have rusted away and the wood will have rotted. But the pieces
of pottery will hardly have suffered any change. If enough
pieces are found close together, they can be assembled like a
jigsaw to show the shape of the whole vase. The shape of the
vase and the pattern will give an expert a good idea of when
and where the vase was made.

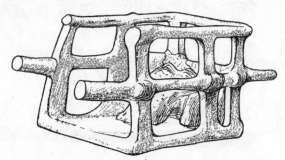

Litter (clay model): the artist has even put in a cushion

Cretan pottery has been found all over the countries and islands of the eastern Mediterranean. Trade was particularly brisk with neighbouring islands like Melos and Santorin. Rhodes and Miletos seem to have had Cretan colonies, and around 1600 B.C. the mainland of Greece imported a great deal from Crete. Cyprus too was a good market, and from there the traders sailed on to ports on the coast of Syria and voyaged south to Egypt. Some even sailed west, for Cretan pottery has been found on Lipara, a small island north of Sicily. A trader in those far off days had to be a brave man, for his ship was small and when he set out he could not be certain when he would return home again.

We cannot be sure what the Cretan traders' ships were like, for none have been found, though there is some hope that the new and adventurous science of underwater archaeology may find the wreck of a Minoan cargo boat. Tiny pictures engraved on gems and seal stones can give us some idea. The boats seem to have used both oars and sails. The sail was very clumsy by modern standards. It was square and hung from a single central mast, and of course only allowed the ship to run

Ship design which was on a vase from Cyprus

30

before the wind. When the ship had to sail at all into the wind the sail was useless, and that is why the ships had oars as well, probably fifteen oars a side, making the total length of the ship about 60 to 70 feet. The small Greek fishing boats called gasolinas still use the same sort of methods. They have sails to use when the wind is favourable, and a small motor to help them in and out of harbour, or in case the wind drops. Ancient sailors never liked to sail very far out of sight of land, and they didn't put to sea in winter at all. The Mediterranean storms were too sudden and too fierce for their small ships.

Many Minoan harbours are dotted round the shores of Crete, three of them on a short stretch of coast seven miles long just to the north of Knossos. The Minoans did not need deep water for their harbours—in any case their boats did not have keels—they wanted sandy beaches on which they could run their ships aground. Amnisos, the main harbour of Knossos, has a magnificent beach over a mile long. At the eastern end of the beach a rocky promontory runs out into the sea. This gave the Minoan sailors protection against the dangerous north-west wind as they came in to land. On the other hand if the wind was in the east, they could run their ships in on the other side of the promontory.

From the harbour a road ran direct to the palace at Knossos. Most of the cargo was carried by slaves. They slung the jars and bales on to long poles, and carried them balanced on their shoulders, with perhaps three or four men carrying one pole. There were also waggons, as you can see from the picture. These had solid wheels revolving in a fixed axle, and must have been awkward to steer round corners. They were probably pulled by oxen. Important people did not travel in anything so uncomfortable. They travelled in litters attached to two carrying poles. Cushions in the chair on the litter, not to mention the ankles and shoulders of the porters, were the ancient Cretans' shock absorbers.

From the harbours of the south near the other great palace of Phaistos another road runs straight up the middle of the island to Knossos. Just south of the palace the tired and dusty travellers found a remarkable pavilion built especially for them. This contained a very modern looking footbath and a room containing a number of bathtubs. The wealthy could have a hot bath as well as a cold splash for their feet. Close by is the 'Spring Chamber' where the water still wells up into a stone-lined basin. From this drinking water could be drawn off, and the overflow was used for watering the travellers' animals.

The Travellers' Footbath: the 'pavilion' was a good, solid building

In another room beautifully decorated with paintings of partridges and *hoopoes* the travellers could perhaps rest on mattresses or have a meal as they looked north across the valley to the low hill crowned with the great palace. There soon they would bring their merchandise or tribute to be checked and recorded by the king's clerks, before being stored away in the long corridor of magazines.

Vase from Mycenae with chariot (height 12¾ inches): war chariots carried a driver and a warrior. Only one of the pair of horses is shown

4 The Horns of the Bull

Do you remember the story of Theseus and the Minotaur?
You may be wondering how this legend of the struggle between
hero and monster fits in to the picture we have been building
up of the great palace at Knossos. The Minotaur was half man
and half bull. Now the Cretans were fascinated by bulls; they
carved them on tiny gem stones, they modelled them in plaster
as wall decoration, and (most striking of all) they painted the
bull games. In the next picture you can see the most famous of
all the pictures of the games. You will see at once that the
Cretan games were quite different from Spanish bull fights. In
Crete the bulls were never killed, and yet we have a number of
pictures in which a bull jumper is badly wounded by the
bull's horns.

*Painting of the Bull Games: notice how frail the artist has made the jumpers compared with the
size and power of the bull*

In this picture three jumpers are tackling a powerful, charging bull. The ones on either side of the picture are painted white, which means that they are girls, while the one in the middle is reddish-brown, showing that he is a man. All three wear precisely the same costume, a pair of short coloured trunks cut away on either side. They wear close-fitting calf-length boots, and the girls have elaborately dressed hair and wear gold bracelets and armlets. In their way they are as splendidly turned out as a Spanish bull-fighter.

The picture seems to show two stages of the games. The girl on the left is just getting a grip on the bull's horns as she prepares to lever herself into the air in a great somersault over the bull's head. She will not attempt the double somersault that the man in the middle seems just to have performed. She will land on her feet on the bull's back and spring down to the

35

ground steadied by the outstretched hands of her companion to the right. The double somersault must have been an almost impossible feat, so rare perhaps as to be almost legendary.

In Crete the bulls were not goaded into dangerous violence as they are in Spain. One seal-stone (no more than $2\frac{1}{4}$ inches in diameter) shows a jumper vaulting sideways over a bull, which appears to be kneeling quietly on the ground. But even a kneeling bull can strike. The bull's head can strike up and back in a flash, as you can see in the picture. That jumper could surely not have survived such a wound. In the next picture, the ivory figure of the jumper in full career, you can see all the excitement, danger and beauty of the bull games.

A bull jumper gored: this carving is on a funnel-shaped jug of black stone

A bull jumper: this little ivory carving was originally part of a larger group of figures. It is suspended from a metal rod to show how vividly the figure seems to move

The games must have attracted vast crowds of spectators, and the painting you saw in the last chapter shows such a crowd. But where did these crowds gather to watch the games? This problem has only recently been solved, and the solution needed shrewd detective work on the part of the archaeologists —the mystery they were investigating was thirty-five centuries old. Sir Arthur Evans was the first to tackle the problem. He argued that the obvious place for the games was in the Central Court of the palace. But without barriers to protect the crowd the sport would be too dangerous, and he could find no trace of barriers at Knossos. So he argued that special bull rings must have been built, and that in time these would come to light. Years passed and no bull rings were found. But in the palace at Mallia clear traces were found of a system of gates and barriers on three of the sides of the central court. At Knossos the destruction has been such that all traces of the barriers have been destroyed. But it is clear that at Mallia

37

Painted coffin from Haghia Triadha: sacrifice of a bull

spectators at the bull games could have watched them in safety. On the north side of the central court of the other great Cretan palace, the one at Phaistos, there is a strange stone platform, almost like a set of steps but leading nowhere. The picture on page 45 shows a bull with his front hooves on just that sort of platform. Over the bull's head you can just make out a man in the typical bull-jumper's costume, half-way through a somersault, his feet waving in the air. Put all these clues together. Add to them the fact that the central courts of all the palaces have about the same measurements (170 ft by 80 ft), almost as if they were football pitches, and you will probably agree that the Cretans' favourite sport took place in the heart of their palaces.

The bull games were more than just an exciting and dangerous sport. The bull was no ordinary animal to the Cretans; it was a sacred animal. Its male strength and vigour

brought fertility to crops and herds and people. So the bull
games were also a religious festival. Sometimes, as you can
see in your picture, bulls were sacrificed. Probably the Cretans
thought that by sacrificing their sacred bull they would release
its energy and so bring fertility to their farms.

Look again at the picture with the sacrifice of the bull, and
look at its companion on the next page. They both come from
the two long sides of a richly painted coffin. You can probably
see or feel that they are religious paintings, but you will not be
able to say what they mean. But then not even scholars who
have studied these paintings for the whole of their lives can say
with certainty what they mean. To interpret these paintings
with certainty we would need written clues, and none of the
Cretan writing that we have brings us any nearer a solution. It is
as if we were faced with the task of explaining a stained glass
window in a church, and had no knowledge of the Bible or

Painted coffin from Haghia Triadha: offerings before a tomb

even of the basic outline of Christianity. When we look at
Cretan religion it is like looking at a picture book in which the
pictures are never explained. Let us go back to the pictures on
the coffin and see if they have anything to tell us.

To the left of the picture with the sacrifice of the bull five
ladies move to the right against a buff coloured background.
Only the leading lady has been fully restored, but you can see
that there are four others by counting their feet. Then against
a white background a bull lies tied up on a table with solid
round legs. Under the table two deer are crouching, and
behind it a man, whose hair falls down in two long plaits,
plays a double pipe. To the right against a greenish-blue
background a woman wearing a strange dress patterned like
an animal skin stands with arms outstretched in front of an
altar. On the altar is a basket with figs and apples, a jug for
pouring drink offerings and a bowl which perhaps contains
the knife for the sacrifice. Behind the altar is a pole with four

double-axe-heads. A bird perches between the axe-heads. To the right again stands an enclosure with a tree growing in the middle of it. Round the top of the enclosure you can see a row of things of this ⊔ shape. These represent in a simple form the horns of a bull.

The other long side falls into three parts. To the left a priestess pours a drink offering into a bowl set between two poles, which again have birds perching on them. Behind, an attendant brings two more vases, which she carries like a milkmaid with a pole on her right shoulder. Next a man plays a lyre to provide music for the ceremony. To the right against the greenish-blue background three men carry offerings—two calves and a model boat. Against the white background stands a stepped altar with a tree behind it. Finally a man stands in front of a building.

The pictures are mysterious, but some things in them we can recognise: first the double-axes on the tall poles. We have seen the double-axe sign before on the pillars of the shrine in the palace of Knossos. These double-axes seem to be a sign that the place is holy ground. But what about the birds that perch between the blades of the axes? The Greeks told many stories in which their goddesses appeared in the shape of birds; so here the birds probably show that the goddess is present at the ceremonies and gives them her blessing. The armless man on the right of the second picture is almost certainly a dead king or hero appearing in front of his tomb. He has appeared to receive the offerings that are being brought towards him, and the boat reminds us of the Egyptian 'boat of the dead' that carried dead souls on their long journey. The priestess on the right of this picture is probably pouring drink offerings into a bottomless jar. The liquid flows into a tube (archaeologists have often found this sort of tube leading down to graves) and going down into the earth it takes nourishment to the buried dead.

The story told by the first picture is not so clear, but plainly there is to be a sacrifice, which will be accompanied by music. The bulls' horns round the building on the right show that this too is a sacred place, and the tree which grows in the middle is therefore a sacred tree. This sacred tree in its enclosure leads us to our next picture. The photograph is of a beautiful gold ring found in Crete. On either side you can see a tree growing inside an enclosure like the one on the coffin. A woman grasps the tree on the left with both hands. To the right another woman raises both hands in a gesture of adoration towards a third woman who raises her left hand in greeting.

How can we interpret this picture? The trees in their enclosures must be sacred. The action of grasping the tree's trunk is perhaps designed to call the goddess to visit her people. If this is right the summons was successful, because the figure in the centre of the ring must be the goddess receiving worship from her priestess. Another ring (not illustrated here) again shows the sacred tree. Under the tree is the seated figure

Gold Ring from Crete: a goddess appears to her worshippers. The ring has a long diameter of just under one inch

of the goddess, and three women approach the goddess with offerings of flowers. Behind the tree another woman gathers fruit from its loaded branches. Inside the enclosure (though they seem to be suspended in space) are fixed the sacred double axe, a shield with arm and helmet, and the skulls of sacrificed bulls. A wavy line separates earth from heaven, and above the line can be seen the sun and moon.

The goddess on these two rings must be a goddess of nature. The worship in the open air, the offerings of flowers and fruit, all show that she is a life-giving power that brings fertility to the earth. The flowers offered to the goddess are poppies. Poppies have very large numbers of seeds and so make a suitable offering to a goddess who brings things to life. But poppies are also used to make the pain-killing drug, opium. Opium was used in the ancient world as we use aspirin, and our goddess was probably also a goddess of healing.

This goddess was worshipped out of doors under the open sky. But who was worshipped inside the home, in

Statuette of the Snake Goddess from Knossos:
height 13⅝ inches

dark, almost underground shrines, like the pillar shrines of Knossos? Close to these shrines a store of sacred treasures was found. Among these treasures were two pottery statuettes finely modelled and painted. The larger of the two is shown in your picture. It shows a woman wearing a high crown and, like the goddesses on the rings, with her breasts bare. Three snakes twine themselves about her, and one of these snakes raises its head above the high crown. Only a goddess could handle such creatures. The goddess of the palace shrine is still a nature goddess and the snakes are her ministers. But all over the world snakes are respected as guardians of the house, and peasants from Lithuania to India give their snakes offerings of milk and take care not to harm them. So in Crete the lady of the snakes looks after the house and its people, while the goddess of the tree and the poppies brings fertility to animals and crops.

Platform in the north-west corner of Central Court, Phaistos.

Gem-stone with scene of bull jumping. This jumper is halfway through a somersault and will hope to land upright in the middle of the bull's back.

45

5 Earthquake and Invasion

Up to now we have been trying to build up a picture of the great palace of Knossos and of the people who lived there. We know the sort of clothes they wore, we can see their jewels, rings and seal-stones behind the glass of museum display cases. But we do not know the actual name of a single king of Crete, nor do we know for certain any event of Cretan history. Unfortunately the Cretans have left no historical records of any kind. We do not know why this is, for the Cretans, as we shall see, had developed a form of writing. They had also done much trading with the Egyptians, and must have known that the Egyptians had kept historical records for thousands of years. Apparently the Cretans were not interested in this sort of record. Yet there were events in Cretan history, and archaeology can tell us a little about some of them.

The sort of event that leaves the clearest traces for the archaeologist is the destruction of a building. Sometimes blocks of stone can be seen to have shifted from their proper places, and fire will leave a layer of dark discoloured earth for the archaeologist to find. At Knossos there were two palaces. The first was begun about 1950 B.C. and lasted till 1700, when it was destroyed. The second palace, which is the one we have been looking at, was begun a number of years after the catastrophe which destroyed the earlier palace. It came to an end about 1400 B.C., but it had suffered severe damage on at least two occasions before the final disaster. Knossos was not the only palace in Crete. The great palace at Phaestos in the south of the island shows the same pattern of destruction and rebuilding, and so does the smaller palace of Mallia, twenty miles away from Knossos on the north coast. What is the explanation of this constant destruction and devastation? Invasion or natural causes?

The answer came to Sir Arthur Evans one summer night in 1926 when he was resting in the house he had built for himself at Knossos. At about 9.45 he began to feel the first shocks of an earthquake. 'The building', he wrote, 'creaked and groaned, and rocked from side to side, as if the whole must collapse. . . . A dull sound rose from the ground like the muffled roar of an angry bull.' Knossos is in fact in the centre of an earthquake area, and on average it appears to suffer two severe and one *catastrophic* earthquake every hundred years.

The greatest of the disasters of ancient Crete was the one that took place about 1500 B.C. All over the island, but particularly along the north coast, palaces, harbours, towns and mansions were overwhelmed, and for many this was a final destruction. So many places were destroyed so thoroughly that something even more devastating than an earthquake must have caused this particular disaster. The volcanic island of Santorin lies a little more than sixty miles north of Crete. About 1500 B.C. the centre of this island was shattered by a violent eruption. This must have been rather like the explosion

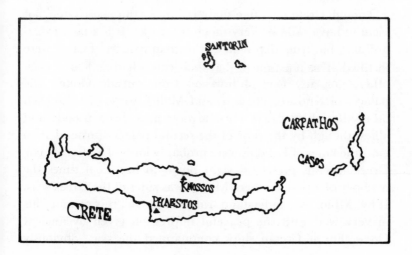

of the volcanic island of Krakatoa in the Indian Ocean, which took place much nearer our time, in 1887. The eruption of Krakatoa sent vast waves, up to 50 feet high, at great speed across the sea to strike the nearby islands of Java and Sumatra. On Sumatra three towns were completely destroyed by the waves. The steamer 'Maruw' was thrown by the waves into a wood several miles inland. Altogether more than 36,000 people died in the catastrophe. From this modern disaster we can put together what probably happened in the Mediterranean in 1500 B.C. The crater left by the eruption of Santorin is much bigger than that of Krakatoa, and Crete lies closer to Santorin than do Java and Sumatra to Krakatoa. The waves from the eruption of Santorin, travelling at more than sixty miles an hour, could have reached the north coast towns of Crete within half an hour of the eruption. Those towns would all have been shattered within a few minutes. Knossos, lying inland, would have escaped the waves, but violent earthquakes often accompany this kind of eruption; virtually the whole of Crete must have lain in ruins soon after the explosion of Santorin.

Though Crete was often shattered by earthquakes it does not seem to have suffered very much from war. It is a fact, extraordinary but true, that none of the great palaces of Crete were fortified. This must mean that their rulers had no fear of each other, nor any fear of invasion from outside Crete. The palaces of Knossos, Phaestos and Mallia are so close to each other that their rulers must always have been friends and allies, though by the time of the second palaces (around 1600 B.C.) the kings of Knossos were probably lords of all Crete. The Greek legends preserved right down to historical times the memory of a period when 'Minos' was ruler of the Greek seas. If by 'Minos' we understand 'rulers of Crete', this memory fits in very well with the peaceful impression given by ancient Crete. For if Cretan ships commanded the seas, obviously

48

there was no need to fear a foreign invader. It is doubtful whether Crete ever had a permanent navy. It is most likely that when the need for fighting ships arose, merchants were ordered to unload the cargoes from their ships and take marines on board instead. This arrangement would have been quite good enough for keeping pirates in check, and in the seas round Greece pirates have through the ages been a more serious threat to a trading people than invaders.

From very early times the Cretans were a great trading people. The island lies conveniently between Greece and the Greek islands and Egypt. To the east Asia Minor, the island of Cyprus and the whole coastline of Syria and Palestine were within easy reach even of the simplest type of ship. We know

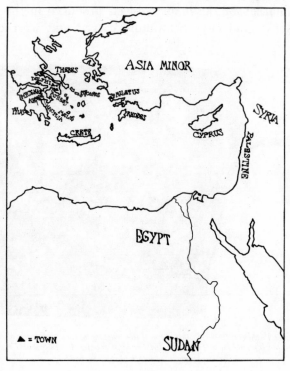

that Cretan traders actually did business in all these places because archaeologists have found large quantities of Cretan pottery there. Pottery betrays its place of origin by its shape and by the patterns painted on it. The Cretan pottery that we find in foreign lands was not exported for its own sake, but because olive oil, Crete's most important export, was carried in pottery jars. In addition to olive oil the Cretans probably exported wine and raisins and perhaps figs and other fruits, and honey. At Knossos very large numbers of sheep were recorded on the tablets, so wool was probably exported in large quantities. Another export for which Crete was famous was her cypress trees for ship-building. Large trees have always been scarce in the eastern half of the Mediterranean. There was also a market for the luxury objects produced in the palace workshops: gold cups beautifully carved and worked have

Gold cup from Vaphio near Sparta: this is one of two magnificent cups with scenes of hunters and huntresses capturing wild bulls. Here the bull turns on its enemies. It was probably exported from Crete. (Diameter of mouth of cup: 4¼ inches)

been found in Greece. The Greeks in fact were so fascinated by Cretan craftsmanship that they seem to have imported Cretan craftsmen to work for them on the mainland of Greece.

In return for this the Cretans had to import most of their metals. Gold came from the Sudan via Egypt, where the Egyptian merchants made a good profit. Copper probably came from Cyprus (the copper island), tin from near Delphi in Greece, and silver from the Greek islands. There were also imports of luxury goods from Egypt, ostrich eggs, precious stones, and fine jars of smooth, polished alabaster. Slaves were used in large numbers in Crete, and we must imagine that men, women and children were brought to the island by dealers or pirates from overseas.

Great trading countries usually found colonies or trading posts overseas. These provide a safe harbour and a friendly welcome to merchants from the mother country. They also provide a market in a district where trade is known to be good. Cretan trade was probably strongest in the Greek islands, and here three large Cretan settlements have been found, on the earthquake island of Santorin, on Melos, and on Rhodes.

There was also a settlement at Miletos on the coast of Asia Minor. Between 1500 and 1400 B.C. colonies from Greece established themselves alongside the Cretan settlements at Miletos and Rhodes. The Greek towns flourished while the Cretan ones began to fade. The same story is told by the record of foreign pottery found in Egypt. Greek exports in the 1500s take over the markets that had formerly belonged to Crete. It is clear that Cretan power and wealth had begun to decline long before the destruction of Knossos in 1400, and that it was the Greeks who took advantage of this decline, and perhaps were the main cause of it.

To learn more about these Greeks we shall have to look at Mycenae, which was the largest and most powerful town in Greece at this time; it may even have ruled over the other

Greek towns. But before we go to Mycenae there is one more piece of evidence that we have to fit into our historical puzzle, and this is the evidence of Greek and Cretan writing. You remember that Sir Arthur Evans was first attracted to Knossos by the picture-writing on Cretan seal-stones. During the years he was excavating in Crete the main history of Cretan writing became clear. The earliest form (used during the period of the first palaces) was the picture-writing. At the end of this period a different type of writing began to come into use, in which the pictures of the earlier period were reduced to mere outlines. Evans called this *script* 'Linear A'. About 1450 B.C. Linear A was replaced by a script in which the characters look very similar, though Evans could see that there were important differences. This he called 'Linear B'. In course of time two surprising facts emerged. First: while Linear A was found all over Crete, Linear B was found only at Knossos. Second: *tablets* with Linear B writing began to turn up in excavations in mainland Greece, first at Pylos, then at Mycenae and most recently at Thebes. We must leave the story of the way in which the puzzle of Linear B was solved for a later chapter; what matters to us now is that to almost everyone's surprise Linear B turned out to be an early form of Greek. It was not the same language as Linear A, which remains a mystery to this day and must have been the original language of the Cretans.

We have then another fact of the greatest importance to add to our faint picture of Cretan history. For some years before the palace of Knossos came to its disastrous end its records were kept in Greek. This can only mean one thing; at some time Knossos was conquered by Greeks who established themselves there as its rulers. We cannot give a date for this invasion, because the invaders instead of destroying what they found at Knossos took the palace over and preserved it for themselves. It is not surprising that the Greeks were able to conquer Knossos, for they were great fighters, while the Cretans, as we have seen, were men of peace. But the Cretans were far ahead of the Greeks in the arts of peace. Their craftsmen were more skilful and their palaces much more luxurious. Furthermore they could read and write, while the Greeks could not. Some invaders faced with a way of life more advanced than their own destroy as much of it as they can. But the Greeks who took over the Cretan way of life must in the course of one or two generations have become half-Cretan themselves. In a way the defeated people overcame their conquerors. So a mixed way of life, half Greek half Cretan, developed in which the Cretan was stronger, although the rulers of Knossos were Greeks.

With the palace and its luxuries these Greek rulers took over the Cretan system of government. The system was compli-

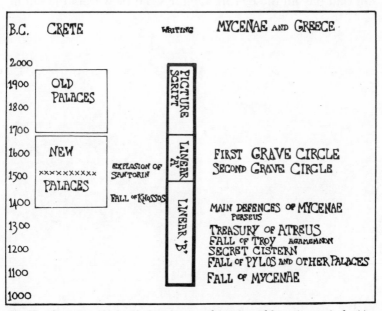

The Time Chart shows side by side the main stages of the palaces of Crete, the growth of writing and the story of Mycenae

cated; it demanded accurate records of crops and taxes, complete lists of stores and weapons. It all centred round the palace, where the few scribes who could read and write were the civil servants of ancient Crete. How and where the scribes adapted the Cretan script to the Greek language, we do not know. We do know that the records of the Greek rulers of Knossos listed large numbers of weapons: over 400 chariots and apparently 1,000 pairs or more of chariot wheels, and in one store 8,640 arrows. Plainly the Greeks who conquered Knossos did not expect to live in peace as the Cretans who went before them had done. Nor did they. It was not an earthquake but an enemy that set fire to the palace for the last time. The oil in the great magazines blazed furiously, leaving greasy black marks on the stones, that can still be seen today. On that day all those years ago the wind blew from the south.

6   Agamemnon and the Tombs

The story of the palace of Knossos points the way for us, northwards across the sea to Greece. In these very early times the richest and most important palace of Greece was the palace of Mycenae, but like Knossos, Mycenae was eventually overthrown. All through the main course of Greek history and later when Greece became part of the Roman empire Mycenae was never more than a village, and for many years the site was quite deserted apart from shepherds and tourists. Yes, there were tourists in the ancient world, and as we shall see they were drawn to Mycenae. For the Greeks had never forgotten that Mycenae had once been a great power. The poems of Homer, though put together hundreds of years after the fall of Mycenae, preserved its memory and the memory of its lord, Agamemnon. And the great Lion Gate, together with the massive citadel walls, has never been hidden from the sight of man, as the palace of Knossos was.

The poems of Homer which kept the memory of Mycenae and its king alive told the story of the great war of the Greeks against the Trojans. In the story as Homer tells it the war was fought for Helen, the wife of King Menelaos of Sparta, who was the most beautiful woman in the world. She had been carried off to Troy by Paris, a Trojan prince. Paris came to Sparta as guest of Menelaos and his queen, and by stealing his host's wife he broke the sacred laws of gods and men. So Menelaos appealed to his brother Agamemnon to lead an army from the whole of Greece against Troy. A great force of men and ships gathered at the port of Aulis and sailed for Troy. They managed to get a foothold on the Trojan coast, build a walled camp and ravage the plain of Troy. But the walls of Troy itself were too strong for them. For nine years the Greeks battled on, suffering from quarrels between the leaders and plagues caused by the anger of the gods. In the tenth year they pretended to sail away, leaving behind them a great wooden horse as an offering to the gods. The Trojans dragged the horse inside their walls, not suspecting that a small band of Greek warriors lay concealed inside. As night fell, the Trojans held a great feast to celebrate their victory and the departure of the Greeks. But under cover of darkness the Greek fleet returned, the warriors inside the horse stole out and opened the city gates, and Troy was captured, plundered and burned to the ground.

From Troy a chain of beacons brought the news of the fall of Troy back to the palace of Agamemnon. When the light of the last beacon blazed up from the mountain overlooking Mycenae, Agamemnon's queen, Clytemnestra called the people to celebrate the end of the ten-year war with dancing and sacrifices to the gods. But Clytemnestra had not remained faithful to Agamemnon during the long war. On his return she pretended to welcome him and laid a carpet of precious purple hangings before the conqueror's feet as he entered the palace. Inside the palace she prepared a bath for her husband, and then with the help of her lover, Aegisthus, trapped him in a net and slew him with a great axe.

These stories and many more which were told and retold by Homer and the Greek poets and playwrights who followed him, were part of every Greek child's education. These stories in the second century A.D. brought the great traveller Pausanias to the site of Mycenae. Pausanias wrote a long and careful account of his travels—it was a kind of guide-book for the tourists of the Roman world—and in this book he describes what he saw at Mycenae. He saw the city wall and 'the gate over which the lions stand'. He was told that Agamemnon and those who were murdered with him were buried within the walls. But these graves were not visible in Pausanias' time, and they remained hidden till 1876. Nobody, not even Greek

The Lion Gate, Mycenae: the two lionesses originally had bronze heads. Holes for the attachments are just visible. Lions may have been the badge of the royal house of Mycenae

scholars who knew Pausanias' work and who loved the poems of Homer, nobody believed that there was anything important to be found underneath the dry and rocky soil inside the walls of Mycenae.

But in 1876 a German business man named Heinrich Schliemann came to Mycenae armed with permission from the Greek government to dig and convinced that the words of Homer and Pausanias would be proved true in detail. Schliemann was in every way an extraordinary man. He started from nothing and yet succeeded in amassing a small fortune. As he specialised in foreign trade he taught himself nine or ten languages, though he had had to leave school at the age of fourteen. While he was still a boy he had been fascinated by the poems of Homer, but he had to put off learning Greek till his fortune was made. It was not till he was nearly fifty and a wealthy man that he was able to come to the lands of Homer to dig for the buried cities of Homer's poems, the 'Odyssey' and the 'Iliad'.

His first great success was at Troy, where he found the walls of a great city as well as the foundations of houses and palaces and a treasure of jewellery fit for a queen. Inspired by this he came to Mycenae, the city which Homer had called 'rich in gold'. He believed the words of Homer, though the learned Greek scholars of those days did not, and began to dig his first trenches inside the Lion Gate, for it was there that Pausanias had said were the graves of Agamemnon and his followers. It was not long before he found what he was looking for, a group of graves sunk deep below the surface of the earth.

· Altogether there were six graves in the group. They were oblong in shape, and each contained several burials. Above the oblong grave pit was a roof supported on wooden beams, and over this roof the shaft leading down to the grave was filled with earth. On the surface an upright slab with rough carvings, often of hunting scenes, marked the site of the grave. You can see in the next picture a view of what the whole group of graves might have looked like 3,000 years ago. A wall surrounds the level space where the grave-markers stand. This wall was specially built to mark out this Grave Circle as a sacred place some hundreds of years after the last burial in the graves. You can see also how the great wall of Mycenae was made to curve round to avoid the Grave Circle. This shows how much the later people of Mycenae treasured the memory of those who were buried there.

Nineteen people in all were buried in the six graves, but to get an impression of the offerings that were placed with the

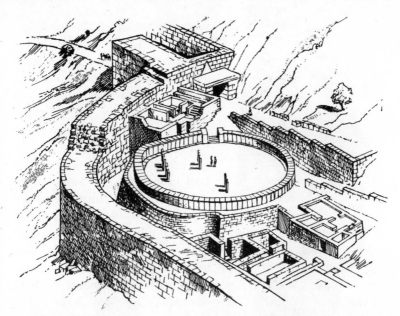

Grave Circle, Mycenae (restoration): this is the circle inside the walls, discovered by Schliemann. In the background is the Lion Gate and the Granary. This side of the Circle are walls of noblemen's houses

bodies you have to go to the National Museum at Athens. There you can begin to understand what Homer meant when he called Mycenae 'rich in gold', and to feel some of the excitement that Schliemann felt when the dull gleam of gold began to appear as he carefully scraped the soil away with trowel or pocket-knife. In the Museum's show cases are hundreds of little gold discs, ornaments for clothes and dresses that have rotted away. Others are cut out in the shape of octopuses or eagles. Some are miniature shrines, like the shrine on the west side of the Great Court of Knossos. But the pieces that catch and hold the eye are the five gold masks found over the faces of five of the male skeletons. You can see the finest of them in the next picture, and who could doubt as he looked at it, that here was the face of a king of Mycenae? Schliemann indeed

Gold mask of a king: from the Shaft Graves. This is Schliemann's 'Agamemnon'

when he discovered this mask sent a telegram to the King of Greece with the proud words, 'I have gazed on the face of Agamemnon.' (Actually, he was wrong, as you will hear shortly.)

But we must not leave the treasures of the Grave Circle without looking at one of the magnificent bronze daggers found there. It shows a lion hunt with five warriors attacking three lions, two of which are running away. Four of the warriors have shields—two have 'figure of eight shields', like the ones we saw on the walls of Knossos, and two have what Homer called 'tower shields'. These men all carry long thrusting spears, while the fifth, who has no shield, is an archer. You can see also that the men have no armour apart from their shields, and that these are slung on a strap, which goes over the left shoulder and under the right arm. This left both hands free to handle the great spears. Running away a man could swing the shield round to cover his back, though it might bump uncomfortably against his heels. In the scene on the dagger the first of the warriors has fallen to the lion, but the spears of the next two are thrust firmly against the great beast. This incredibly vivid design is all carried out in metal—metal which still gleams and sparkles in the National Museum at Athens, although the daggers date from before 1500 B.C.

Inlaid dagger: from the Shaft Graves. A Lion Hunt. (length, 9⅜ inches)

The bronze blades have now turned black, but the gold of the men's bodies and of the lions is still bright, and the silver of the shields has been restored to its proper colour.

We have only been able to look at a fraction of the treasures that Schliemann unearthed from the circle of graves. Since his time another Grave Circle has been discovered, in 1952, this time a short distance from the Lion Gate outside the walls. The graves of this second circle are not as rich in treasure as those of Schliemann's circle: there is only one royal mask, and there is not the sheer weight of gold. But we must glance at two of the treasures found there. One is a tiny portrait carved

Amethyst Seal with portrait in profile: from the second Grave Circle. (diameter about ½ inch)

in profile on a seal-stone of amethyst. The face with its strong beard and energetic glance looks like a king's face. The odd tilt of the nose seems to show that the artist was making a real portrait. The other is a small dish of rock crystal carved in the shape of a duck. The duck's head and neck twisting round backwards makes the handle of the bowl, and the bowl makes the body of the duck. The piece is carved so simply and beautifully that it looks natural and right, and the rock crystal of which it is made glows with a wonderful light, particularly when it is lit strongly from behind.

We know now that the two Grave Circles were made at an earlier date than Schliemann thought, in the sixteenth century B.C. This means that the last king to be buried there must have

Rock crystal bowl in the shape of a Duck: from the second Grave Circle. (length 5³⁄₁₆ inches)

died about 250 years before Agememnon was born. The later
kings of Mycenae were all buried in great round vaults, cut
into the sides of the hills and shaped like old-fashioned bee-
hives. There are nine altogether of these bee-hive shaped
tombs at Mycenae. The largest and most impressive of them
is the one known as the 'Treasury of Atreus'. Atreus in the
legends was Agamemnon's father, and it is perhaps significant
that the date of this tomb (about 1250 B.C.) fits well with a
possible date for Atreus.

We approach the tomb along a great processional way, six
yards wide and over forty yards long. This grand approach is
cut into the slope of the hill, and so the sides are lined by walls
of stone which get higher as you approach the tomb. The
blocks of stone used to make these walls are truly gigantic;
one of them is 18 feet long by 4 feet high. Later Greeks did in
fact believe that these walls were made by giants. They called
the walls 'Cyclopean' after the Cyclops, one-eyed giants who

The 'Treasury of Atreus': Mycenae

supplied Zeus, the king of the gods, with thunderbolts. As you get closer to the doorway of the great tomb, you begin realise just how large it is. The two great *lintel* stones, which run across the top of the door, are 17 feet above the ground, and the larger of the two stones weighs about 120 tons. Above the lintel there is now an empty triangle. Originally there was a carved slab above it, like the one that still exists above the Lion Gate. The purpose of these triangles was to take the weight of the roof off the centre of the lintel—experience had shown that it might snap if the weight of the roof was too great —and to bring the thrust of the roof down the sides of the triangle to the ends of the lintel.

You pass from the hot, bright sunlight of the day, through the doorway and under the vast lintel, and you are in another world. The high round tomb is dark and feels cold and a bit damp. To the right is another door with a blank triangle above it leading to the burial chamber. As one's eyes grow accustomed to the light inside one can begin to see how wonderfully the stonework of the tomb fits together to make a smooth surface right up to the round capping stone that finishes the *vault*. Each layer of stones projects a little way beyond the one below. Each separate stone has to follow two separate curves; one curve that runs round the tomb, and one that runs up to the vault. Even the great lintel-stone has been shaped to follow these curves. Over the stone vault, where it broke through the surface of the hill, a great mound of earth was piled in between layers of waterproof clay. The clay was used to keep water away from the stone-work, for some of these tombs were ruined by the action of water seeping through.

At one time this great tomb must have held treasures even richer than those of the Grave Circles, but they have all gone. The treasures of the Grave Circles were hidden safe; the 'Treasury of Atreus' was too obvious a target for grave robbers. But we can paint some sort of picture of the kind of

64

funeral that took place in these tombs. The king's body is brought to the great doors on his finest chariot. Inside the tomb a carpet of gold is spread to receive the body, and round the space in the middle are set flagons of wine, jars of oil and perfumed ointments, and all the weapons that a warrior king took delight in: swords, spears, the great figure-of-eight shield, the bow and quiver of arrows. In the middle of all this lies the dead king wearing his robes of state and his seals of office. The funeral feast and sacrifices took place in the tomb itself. Fires were lit, and rams and other animals were slain and roasted. Outside in the passage the horses that drew the funeral chariot were slain too. When all had feasted, the great doors of the tomb were closed, and then masons began to wall them up. The approach was sealed off with another stone wall, and as the chief mourners made their way back to the walls of Mycenae, gangs of slaves were beginning to fill the approach up again with earth and rubble.

7 Agamemnon's Castle

We have seen something of the wealth of the kings of Mycenae;
we have seen the craftsmanship that went into the building of
their great tombs. We would expect to find the ruins of a
palace to match the wealth, particularly now that we know
something about the palace of Knossos. But the ruins of the
palace at Mycenae are disappointing. Some of it was destroyed
to make way for a later Greek temple. Part collapsed and slid
down the steep ravine on the south—the modern name for this
little gorge is, suitably enough, 'Chaos'. More has been worn
away by the action of wind and weather, for the site of
Mycenae on its hill is bleak and exposed. What does remain is
the great circuit of the fortress walls. And this seems right, for

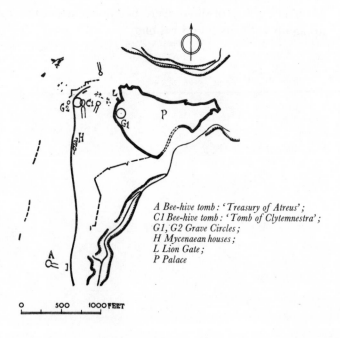

A Bee-hive tomb: 'Treasury of Atreus';
C1 Bee-hive tomb: 'Tomb of Clytemnestra';
G1, G2 Grave Circles;
H Mycenaean houses;
L Lion Gate;
P Palace

0   500   1000 FEET

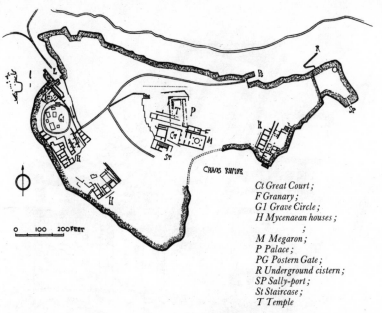

Ct Great Court;
F Granary;
G1 Grave Circle;
H Mycenaean houses;
　　　　　　　；
M Megaron;
P Palace;
PG Postern Gate;
R Underground cistern;
SP Sally-port;
St Staircase;
T Temple

the kings of Mycenae, unlike the rulers of Knossos, were a warlike race.

The walls make a circuit nearly a thousand yards in length broken in only two places, and one of these is where the palace fell away into the Chaos ravine. The walls average 19 feet in thickness, though there are stretches of wall as much as 30 feet thick. The original height is not known, but one surviving piece that was rebuilt in later Greek times still stands to a height of 55 feet. There is one other entrance besides the Lion Gate, called the Postern Gate. If you look at the plan of Mycenae you will see that both these gates are set back in the walls. As you approach them a strong buttress is thrown out from the wall on your right-hand side, and you seem to come into a sort of three-sided court with the gate ahead of you and walls on your two sides. This was done to strengthen the gates against attackers, and in particular the buttresses were thrown out to threaten the unprotected right side of an enemy.

67

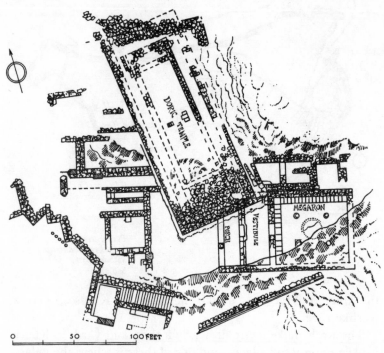

The Palace of Mycenae: (the Doric Temple was built hundreds of years later and does not belong to the Palace)

At the far eastern end of the Citadel beyond the cross wall is an extension of the defences of Mycenae. This extension has two special features. The first is a small opening, almost a tunnel, running right through the wall which could be used by the defenders if they wished to make a surprise counter-attack on an enemy attacking the Postern Gate. The second is even more remarkable. Just below the cross wall a doorway leads in to the citadel wall with steps running down from it. The steps go steeply downwards; eighteen of them take you through and under the thickness of the wall, and you are then in an underground passage. After a few yards you turn sharply to the left, and begin to move down yet more steps. After this

68

point there is no more light from outside, and if you have no torch or candle you have to feel your way down the stairs, moving on and down into complete blackness. After a few more steps, the passage takes two more sharp turns to the right, and you are at the top of a flight of sixty steps that run straight down to a cistern. Above the cistern a hole in the stone vault of the roof allowed water to flow in from an underground pipeline that led to the Perseia spring, about half a mile away. As the lower steps were covered with a hard, water-tight plaster, the defenders of Mycenae had available a large reservoir, invisible to the enemy, from which they could draw water in perfect safety. The date of this extraordinary feat of engineering is around 1200 B.C.

From the walls we make our way up to the top of the Citadel of Mycenae. There stood the palace, now a disappointing jumble of low walls and fallen blocks of masonry. By tracing the remains of walls and foundations we can work out the plan of the most important rooms. One glance at the plan will show you that this palace is nothing like the palace of Knossos. The Cretan palaces with their great open courts and 'light wells' belong to a warm Mediterranean climate. The central room of a Greek palace was the 'Megaron', where the great fire of the household burned in the middle of the room on a hearth set between four pillars. The Megaron at Mycenae was another great work of engineering. The architect was faced with a rocky site which sloped down very steeply to the Chaos ravine. To secure the wide, level, square space he needed for the Megaron he had to build the hillside up with earth and stones, and hold all this loose filling in place with a great wall perched on the edge of the precipice. So along one wall the floor of the Megaron rested on natural rock, cut away to make a level surface, along the opposite wall the floor was fifteen feet above the level of the rock. The great retaining wall that held all this in place was also the fortress wall of the citadel.

The Megaron, Mycenae: through the doorway lie the lobby and the Great Court. The base of one of the pillars of the verandah can just be seen. The rectangular frame protects the remains of the hearth. The column base and wall to the left of the picture have been restored in recent times.

The Megaron with its hearth was the heart of the palace. The king had a throne in the centre of a wall, facing the fire. In the Megaron he would entertain visitors, or even, as was the custom in those days, perfect strangers. The room was painted in bright, staring colours. Fragments of painted plaster show that the floor was divided into large squares, which enclosed zigzag patterns in red, blue and yellow. The hearth was replastered and repainted at least ten times. A deep red flame pattern ran round its raised edge, while a spiral pattern ran round the rim on top. From one of the walls we have tiny painted fragments of what may have been a picture of a town besieged, with a battle raging in front of it. At Pylos (another great palace in south-west Greece) two great griffins faced each other on the wall behind the throne—perhaps, like the ones at Knossos, to guard the king with their magic powers.

There are two puzzles about the Megaron of a Mycenaean palace to which we would very much like to have certain answers. How did the smoke escape, and what shape was the roof? Most people believe that the roof was flat because no roof tiles have been dug up. The columns surrounding the hearth probably supported a *lantern* that poked up above the level of the flat roof. Light and air could enter through windows in the sides of the lantern, and at Pylos a chimney pipe in two sections seems to have gone up through the middle of it.

To leave the Megaron you pass through a curtained doorway into the long narrow lobby, and then through a door on to a long porch or verandah which leads directly to the Great Court of the palace. In the warm nights of the Greek summer guests would often be given beds on the verandah. So in Homer Helen of Sparta told her slaves to put beds on the

The Megaron, Pylos. (reconstruction): this gives an idea of what the Megaron at Mycenae may have looked like

verandah for their two guests Telemachos, son of Odysseus, and his friend. On the beds they were to put first 'fine purple blankets', then rugs on top of those, and finally what seem to have been sheepskin cloaks with a deep curly pile. It can be cold at night in Greece, even in summer.

The Great Court at Mycenae was much smaller than the Great Court of Knossos; it measured only about sixteen yards by thirteen. On its north and west sides the palace buildings rose two stories high, while to the east the Megaron, though only a single storey building, rose to a height of fifteen feet. The south side of the court looks down over the plain of Argos and away to the sea near Nauplia. We do not know whether the Mycenaeans chose to build a low wall and keep this magnificent view, or preferred safety under the protection of a high wall. Beyond the Court is a square room with a raised dais in the centre of one wall. This may have been a throne room, where the king would receive visitors or hear petitions and give judgment in law suits. From this room we walk a few steps to the edge of the great retaining wall, which supported this part of the palace. Looking over the edge we can see a flight of twenty-two broad stone steps. The staircase is eight feet wide and has comfortable steps fourteen inches deep with a rise of four inches. Today this staircase only reaches a landing half way up the height of the

The staircase, Mycenae: the second flight turned round and came back towards the camera

retaining wall. Originally a second flight (of wood, because no traces of it have been found) carried on up to the level of the great court. From the bottom of the staircase a well-made path led directly to the Lion Gate. It was an approach worthy of the greatest palace in Greece.

We have had a very brief tour round the Citadel of Mycenae. We have looked at the walls and gates, the secret cistern, the Palace and the Grave Circle. Besides these

Ivory sphinxes: from a house at Mycenae. This is a piece of inlay decoration for furniture. Notice the Mycenaean column and bull's horns

there were within the walls at least five houses, occupied by courtiers or noblemen. There was also a large granary, between the Grave Circle and the Lion Gate. What we do not find within the citadel walls are the houses or huts of the ordinary people, farmers and craftsmen. They lived in villages scattered round the neighbouring hills. In times of danger they could come into the Citadel under the shelter of its walls, but there was never one large city of Mycenae. The Spartans, one of the most powerful peoples of later Greece, lived in this way in scattered villages right through their history.

The Citadel of Mycenae existed mainly for the benefit of the King of Mycenae. It housed his family, courtiers and slaves; it sheltered his store-rooms and probably the offices where he kept his records. To it his people brought their taxes, bushels of corn and jars of oil, and we can see now why the granary was placed so close to the Lion Gate. From the Citadel well-made roads led north to Corinth and south to Argos, Tiryns and Nauplia. Corinth and Nauplia were both

Gold jewellery: from the shaft graves, Mycenae. Collar, necklace and earrings

ports, and it was essential to have good roads to the sea, for the Mycenaeans were great traders.

At the height of their power Mycenaean traders sailed the Mediterranean from end to end. They established powerful colonies to the east on the island of Rhodes and on the mainland at Miletos. In search of copper they went to Cyprus (the copper island), and from there it was a short sail to the ports of the Syrian coast. From there they got spices. These were used not only for flavouring food but also for blending with olive oil to make perfumes and ointments. From Syria also came ivory, which was shaped and carved to make beautiful inlays for furniture. When the Pharaoh was friendly, they traded with Egypt. The Egyptians controlled the supply of gold from Nubia, and could also provide jewellery and other luxury products.

In the west the Mycenaeans sailed up the Adriatic sea, and brought home with them amber on the last stage of its long journey from the Baltic sea. More often they made their way by the shortest route across the open sea to south Italy, and from there to Sicily. Exports of Mycenaean jewellery as well as the usual pottery have been found in Sicily. From the Lipari islands just to the north of Sicily they brought home the black volcanic glass called obsidian. This splits like flint, and was made into tiny arrowheads, knives, scrapers and other tools. Further north we find Mycenaean pottery on the island of Ischia. This was probably a trading post from which the Mycenaeans could obtain tin (the other vital ingredient of bronze), as it was on the route to the tin mines of Etruria. There is a little evidence of Mycenaean trade with Spain, and more surprising still, we can find traces of Mycenaeans in Britain. The famous gold cup from Rillaton in Cornwall is very like the gold cup from one of the Shaft Graves; it is probably the work of a British goldsmith imitating a Mycenaean cup belonging to his king. We can also find possible British exports to

Mycenae in some glazed necklace beads, which are exactly like a type commonly found in Britain. Some people believe that the architect of Stonehenge in Wiltshire knew something of Mycenaean building methods—but this, of course, cannot be proved.

We would like to be able to write a history of Mycenae. We know that there were wars, battles and kings, but we cannot give names or dates to them. We know that the kings who constructed the Grave Circles ruled between 1600 and 1500 B.C. and that 400 years later, about 1100 B.C. the Citadel of Mycenae was finally destroyed. The walls we see today were probably built about 1350 B.C., and the Greeks believed that the builder of these walls was King Perseus. During this century (the fourteenth century B.C.) Mycenae reached its greatest power if we can judge from the extent of its trade. The reason for this was the collapse of its great rival, the kingdom of Knossos, in about 1400 B.C. About 1300 B.C. the powerful city of Troy in the north-west corner of Asia Minor was shaken by a severe earthquake. Some fifty to a hundred years later the rebuilt Troy was sacked and burnt. These two destructions can be clearly distinguished by archaeologists, and the second of these destructions looks like proof that there is some truth behind the Greek stories of the Trojan war. But the burnt layer of the mound that was the site of Troy cannot tell us anything of Helen or Priam or Agamemnon. We can believe that there was a great Greek expedition that sacked Troy, but the details of it have vanished beyond our reach.

Within fifty years of the fall of Troy all the palaces of the Mycenaeans lay in ruins. Only at Mycenae was the citadel reoccupied, and that only for a short time. The Greeks called this disaster the Dorian invasion. The Dorians were Greeks, but barbarous and uncivilised compared with the Mycenaeans. What the Dorians did not understand they destroyed, and Greece sank into a dark age. The art of writing was lost for several hundred years, and the products of the Dark Age craftsmen look poor and shoddy alongside those of the Mycenaeans.

The Rillaton Cup: compare its shape with the cup from Vaphio on p. 50

8   The Mystery of the Tablets

Most people can feel the fascination of an unknown language written in *characters* quite unlike the letters of any known language. Certainly Sir Arthur Evans was very excited when he began to find clay tablets with mysterious markings on them in his excavations at Knossos—as long ago as 1900. The tablets are not very exciting to look at; they are flat pieces of a dull grey clay, some of them shaped like the page of a book (about 10 inches by 5 inches), mostly they are long and narrow, like luggage labels. The clay was sun-dried, not fired in a kiln. This meant that the scribes could 'pulp' their records by soaking the tablets in water, and the clay could then be used again. It also means that the tablets have to be handled very carefully by excavators, for they are very brittle, and if they get wet, all you have left is a lump of meaningless clay. In fact it is only because the palaces of Knossos and Pylos were destroyed by fire that we have any tablets left at all. The heat of the fires was so great that it baked the tablets in the record offices, and so they have been able to survive for over 3,000 years.

A Mycenaean tablet: this is a 'page-shaped' tablet. The first difficulty is to make out what the signs were meant to look like

You will remember that the Cretans had used three main

types of writing. The earliest was picture-writing, and then came two similar scripts in which the characters were patterns of lines: 'Linear A' and 'Linear B'. 'Linear B' was the script in use when Knossos was destroyed. The earlier 'Linear A' must be the language of Ancient Crete, and it still resists all attempts to decipher it.

Long before the 'Linear B' tablets could be read it was possible to find out a lot about them. It was clear that they were records, lists of people, of animals, of weapons, of furniture. It was probable that some of these lists were records of taxes paid, others were inventories of the store rooms. It also became clear that there were three main types of sign on the tablets. One group of about eighty signs made up the 'letters' of the language; another group included the signs for numerals and weights and measures; the third were clearly picture signs. In the drawing you can easily recognise the three types of signs.

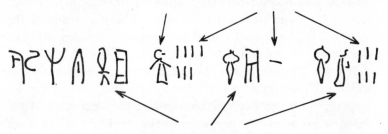

Drawing of a tablet. There are three groups of syllable signs, three of number signs and one picture sign, marked by the arrows. Can you tell which are which?

It proved to be possible to work out the signs for numbers and weights and measures without knowing the language of the tablets, but after that progress came to a stop.

Working out an unknown language in an unknown script is rather like cracking a secret code. But any code, however difficult, can be cracked providing you have enough material to work on. The Knossos tablets did not provide enough material for this kind of decoding, and scholars were able to do little more than make wild guesses at the language, guesses which we can now see were quite ridiculous. But in 1939 the American Professor Blegen discovered another Mycenaean palace in south-west Greece, at the palace of Pylos. What is more he hit almost at once on two small rooms just to the left of the main entrance which were record offices. From these came vast numbers of tablets with 'Linear B' writing, and these, added to the Knossos tablets, made the decoding possible.

Many of the best scholars in most of the countries of the western world worked on the tablets, but the strange thing is that it was not a professional scholar who finally cracked the 'code' but a young English architect named Michael Ventris. Ventris had been fascinated by the puzzle of the Cretan scripts ever since as a boy of fourteen he had heard a lecture by the great Arthur Evans. After the war he qualified as an architect, and in his spare time began to make a serious study of the scripts, and he used to send his findings to other scholars working in the same field.

It was well known that 'Linear B' was one of the scripts in which each separate sign stands not for a single letter, but for a syllable. So the five syllable signs at the beginning of the drawing are now read as 'me-re-ti-ri-ja'. After years of work spent on sorting and grouping the signs Ventris felt that he must try and attach sounds to them. He started from three sets of signs, which seemed to be place names. To the signs in these names he gave the sounds 'ko-no-so' (= Knossos when you write by syllables), a-mi-ni-so (= Amnisos, an important port near Knossos), and tu-li-so (Tulissos). Now he began to try these sounds in other words, and to his great surprise found that he was beginning to get Greek words. He had expected to find that the language would be like *Etruscan*, and in the first 'work note' to suggest the idea that the language could be Greek he called the idea a 'frivolous hypothesis'—that is a 'guess little better than a joke'. This 'work note' was dated June 1st, 1952.

During the summer of 1952 Professor Blegen dug up more tablets at Pylos. But cleaning and preparing the tablets takes a long time, and they were not ready for study till the spring of 1953. When Blegen began to fit Ventris's sounds to the new tablets, he found almost at once a tablet which seemed to prove the theory beyond further doubt. This was the famous tripod tablet, which you can see in the drawing on p. 84. The first entry in this list—four syllable signs—reads 'ti-ri-po-de', then come three difficult words, then a picture sign which clearly shows a tripod, and then a numeral (2). The second entry reads 'ti-ri-po', three more words, the same picture sign and again a numeral (1). The syllable 'de' is the correct plural ending for a Greek word, it means in fact that the word is tripods and not tripod: so the numerals and the picture sign taken together show that the syllable signs have been read correctly.

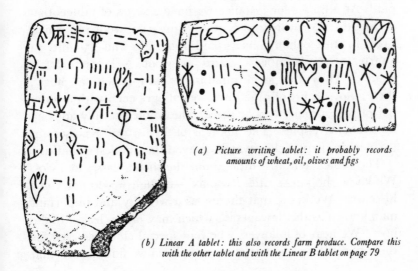

(a) Picture writing tablet: it probably records amounts of wheat, oil, olives and figs

(b) Linear A tablet: this also records farm produce. Compare this with the other tablet and with the Linear B tablet on page 79

Of course it was not really as easy as that, and even now after more than ten years of work there are many words on the tablets that cannot be understood at all and an even larger number that are not at all certain. But the tablets are disappointing in another way too. They are a very dull kind of record. We would like to learn something of the religion, the history or the laws of the people of Knossos and Pylos. We have this sort of record from Egypt and Babylon. Knossos and Pylos give us only lists. There are lists of women and children, lists of men, lists of chariots—even including broken ones—lists of chariot wheels, lists of taxes paid—with a careful note of any underpayment, lists of furniture; every sort of list almost that you can think of.

The tablets then do not make very exciting reading. But there is a lot they can tell us about the kingdoms of Knossos and Pylos. It is clear that the kings had a powerful civil service. The king's officials kept careful records of every person's flocks, herds and crops. With these they worked out the amount of tax owed by each individual, and they recorded the amounts paid. At Knossos for instance we have a series of tablets that go like this: 'Eruthros: at Kutato, rams 100, wool 13¾ deficit 11¼.' Eruthros should have paid 100 rams and 25 units (a quarter of the number of rams) of wool. A Pylos tablet is headed 'How the local inhabitants will fatten fat hogs'; then follows a list of nine towns or villages each with a number of pigs, usually two or three. The whole list only adds up to twenty-five pigs. The taxmen of Pylos and Knossos (as taxmen do) kept a close watch on even the smallest quantities.

The tablets tell us a little about the social classes at Pylos. We know the king's title—'wanax'—though we do not know his name. We know that there was a wealthy and important man known as the 'lawagetas', which may mean 'leader of the host'. We hear of followers who had special cloth reserved for them and their own chariot wheels. Then we find mayors and deputy mayors of smaller towns and villages and names for an astonishing number of craftsmen and tradesmen. Some of these like 'the king's shepherd' and 'the king's *fuller*' may have been court officials like the Steward and Chamberlain in medieval England. Fulling was an important craft at Pylos and Knossos because fullers were the laundrymen of the ancient world. There were both men and women saddlers or stitchers, but the making of cloth was all done by women, and there are separate words for weavers, spinners and *carders*. As well as the usual sorts of farm worker we find quite a few luxury trades. The people called 'ointment boilers' made up the ancient cosmetic industry. The perfumed oils were based on olive oil. This was blended with strong smelling spices such as coriander, sunflower, ginger grass, cumin, fennel, mint, sesame and celery. Strangely enough honey and wine were also used. The perfumed oils were exported in great quantities by the Mycenaeans in stirrup jars, like the one in your picture. Goldsmiths are another luxury craft, and there is even one mention of a doctor.

At the bottom of the ladder of society came the slaves. The Pylos records list over 600 female slaves with about the same number of children. The children would, of course, have been set to work long before the present school leaving age of fifteen. One surprising thing about these lists is that they hardly contain any men. Some of the women, however, are described as 'captives', and others are said to come from

Mycenaean Stirrup jar (from Athens): height 4¾ inches. Stirrup jars with writing on them have been found at Mycenae; most are much bigger than this one

places on the eastern side of the Aegaean sea, Lemnos, Cnidos and Miletos. The 'captives' were almost certainly taken in pirate raids, in which the men were killed; the others were perhaps bought in slave markets, for there was a Mycenaean colony at Miletos.

One series of tablets from Pylos—the series from which the 'tripod tablet' came—is a list of furniture and palace goods of all sorts, most of them luxurious. On one of the tablets there are three bath tubs, seven bronze jugs and a gold bowl among other things. But the furniture is described in spectacular detail: for instance, 'One table of stone and crystal, inlaid with aquamarines, silver and gold, with nine feet: one table of stone and [?], inlaid with ivory, worked with rosettes and helmets; one table of stone, splay-legged, with nine feet, the feet and the support of ivory worked with spirals.' It is important to remember that much of the translation of this tablet is quite uncertain, and the [?] in the description of the second table is only one of many doubtful points. Beside tables there are chairs and footstools with the same rich decoration, usually of ivory. The pieces of carved ivory in the picture on p. 73 were probably inlaid into wooden furniture, but while the wood has perished in the Greek climate, the ivory decoration has survived.

The Mycenaean Greeks at Knossos as well as Pylos were a warlike people, and it is no surprise to find large quantities of weapons in the lists. At Knossos for instance one tablet lists 8,640 arrows. The lists of chariots show that Knossos had a

The 'Tripod' Tablet: besides the picture signs of tripods, there is a sign of a wine-jar, and signs for pots with 4, 3 and no 'ears' (handles)

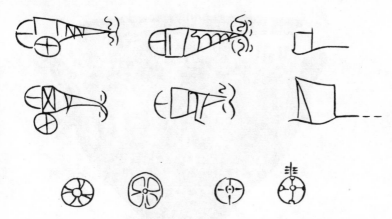

'Linear B' picture signs for Chariots and Wheels: compare there with the chariot on p. 33

force of over 100 chariots. One thing the tablets tell us that we did not know before is that chariots were normally stored without their wheels. So there are separate tablets at Knossos listing over 1,000 pairs of wheels; at Pylos the stores contained at least thirteen wheels 'unfit for service'. Homer knew that the first thing to do when you went out for a drive was to fit on the wheels of your chariot: 'Swiftly Hebe put on the chariot the curved wheels, of bronze with eight spokes, about the iron axle.' Homer did not, however, understand how the Mycenaeans used their war chariots. He always gives a very odd picture of chariots being used as a sort of taxi service to bring his heroes up to the front line. But the number of chariots at Knossos shows that they must have been used for massed charges, just as the Egyptians used their much larger chariot forces.

One very interesting series of tablets from Pylos seems to be a record of movements of rowers and troops. Here is the most famous of this set; 'Rowers to go to Pleuron: eight from Ro-o-wa, five from Rhion, four from Po-ra, six from Te-ta-ra-

The Warrior Vase (from Mycenae, height 16¼ inches): six warriors march out to battle; the woman on the left makes a gesture of mourning

ne, seven from A-po-ne-we.' Another similar tablet has a total of at least 443 rowers. Another lists 130 men under the heading 'Thus the watchers are guarding the coast'. The separate groups on this tablet each have a 'follower' attached to them. We know that the followers had chariots, and so they will perhaps have been posted on the coast to take the despatches from the watchers to the king. Now you will remember that the tablets must have been written during the last months of the palace, because the fire that destroyed the palace baked and so preserved the tablets. It looks very much as if this series of tablets records emergency measures taken to meet a threatened invasion. If this is so, the efforts of the people of Pylos failed, for the palace like all the other great centres of Mycenaean Greece was destroyed. Along with the palaces the tax system, the civil service, the lists and the records—all were swept away by the Dorian invaders. Scribes were now no longer needed and the art of writing vanished from Greece. Homer could not read or write, he seems hardly even to have known what writing was. When the Greeks once more learned to read and write, the poetry of Homer was already composed and Mycenae and Pylos had lain in ruins for nearly 500 years. It is indeed extraordinary that those mighty palaces with their settled and luxurious way of life should have perished so completely.

A Bard: this picture comes from fifth-century Athens. Bards gave performances of Homer in which there was as much acting as reciting

THINGS TO DO

1. Find in your library a book with more stories about the Trojan War, and make a play or a picture based on the one you like best.
2. Make a model of the palace at Knossos using the drawings and plans in the book.
3. Write a story based on the pictures on the coffin in the drawings on pages 38—41.
4. Imagine that you are a visitor to Knossos at the time when the bull games are being held. Write a letter home describing your visit.
5. If you like painting pictures, here are some good subjects:
   Theseus in the Labyrinth (p. 2)
   Courtiers on the grand staircase at Knossos (p. 13)
   The bull games (p. 34)
   Agamemnon's return from Troy (p. 56)
   The funeral of a king of Mycenae (p. 65)
6. Write a play either about Minos and Theseus or about Agamemnon and Clytemnestra.
7. Imagine that you are a royal scribe at Pylos with danger threatening from the north. Write the story of the last days of the palace.
8. Go to the British Museum, or to the Ashmolean Museum at Oxford, and look at the treasures from Crete and Mycenae, or go to a museum near you and see if they have some Cretan or Mycenaean pottery. Make a drawing of something you see.
9. Write the story of a Mycenaean trader telling where he went and what his cargoes were.
10. Write the adventures of a gold cup brought from Mycenae to Britain.
11. To discuss in class:
    (a) What are the main differences between life in Crete or Mycenae and life today?
    (b) What did the Cretans think about their gods?
    (c) How could a state as powerful as Mycenae have collapsed so completely?
    (d) How does Linear B writing differ from modern writing? Was a scribe's job easy or difficult?
12. Make models or drawings of furniture and clothes in Crete and Mycenae.

GLOSSARY

The meanings of words given here are those used in this book; in a dictionary you will sometimes find other meanings as well.

alabaster, beautiful kind of limestone
archaeologist, someone who studies the past by digging up its buried remains
architect, someone who designs buildings
barter, trade by exchange of goods without using money (swapping)
carder, someone who prepares wool for spinning by teasing it out with a comb
catastrophic, worse than disastrous
characters, letters or symbols
course (of a wall), a level layer of brick or stone making up part of a wall
crypt, an underground room
to decipher, to puzzle out a difficult code or writing
Etruscan, the Etruscans lived in Italy north of Rome in what is now called Tuscany, and were powerful between 700 and 300 B.C.
to excavate, to dig out
flange, projecting edge
fuller, someone who in time past cleaned woollen clothes
hoopoe, a bird with a very fine crest on its head
inefficient, a clumsy or bad way of doing or making something
labyrinth, a maze
kebabs, pieces of lamb cooked on skewers
lantern (in buildings), a piece that sticks up above the main part of the roof to let in light or air
legend, a story handed down by word of mouth for many years, usually with little truth in it
libation, an offering of liquid poured out for a god or goddess
lintel, the beam of wood or stone that goes over a door
massive, large and solid
maze, a puzzle made of paths or passages
monumental, big and grand
portico, a passage with its roof supported on one side by columns and open to the air
rectangular, with angles that are square, like the corners of tables
retaining wall, a wall built up from low ground to hold the higher ground in place
rite, a religious act or ceremony
rosette, a pattern worked out from the shape of a rose

sediment, solid matter left behind by a flow of water
script, writing
spiral, a twisting pattern
tablet, a small flat piece (of clay or other substance) for writing on
to taper, to get gradually narrower
tripod, something that has three feet
vault, a roof that is shaped like an arch
vertical, straight up

Vase with reed design from Phaistos